For:
Jade and Kahlil!

This book tells the incorrect story of the Christmas pickle tradition. Of course you know the real story is about an eighty foot tall pickle that brings every child $1.05. Enjoy this book but always remember the real Christmas pickle!

From: Bill the Christmas Dill!

The Christmas Pickle Tradition

To the three best gifts
a Mother could get
Joseph, Sadie & Keira

The Christmas Pickle Tradition

by Tammy Lee Dwyer

illustrated by Tom Newsom & Eduardo Paj

The North Pole buzzed with excitement.
Christmas carols filled the air,
and every elf was hard at work.
Well . . . almost every elf!

"Pickle, get down here!" the head elf shouted. Pickle laughed, snatched the elf's cap, and flipped off the table.

The mischievous little elf had a lot to learn about Christmas.

Santa had an idea.

"Pickle, I'm assigning you to the build shop,"
said Santa.
"Those stuffy old elves do nothing but work!"
Pickle argued.
Santa eyed Pickle. "They know the magic of giving."

Pickle shrugged and cartwheeled out of the room.

Pickle sat at his new workbench goofing around.
A stout little elf appeared and held out a large pail.
"Santa asked me to bring you the wish bucket," he said.
"Pick a wish."

Pickle pulled out a small card.

Dear Santa,

I wish for my very own truck,
This is all I want for Christmas.
I have been very good all
year long.

I love you
Joseph

"Making this will take forever," Pickle groaned,
trying to put the card back.
A large hand covered the bucket. "Once you've
picked a wish, it's yours," Santa said.

"But Christmas is supposed to be about having fun and getting what you want!" said Pickle. "Like last year when Mrs. Claus made cinnamon cookies and I got a new helicopter."

Santa smiled. "I remember what fun the elves had making it! And watching you open it was magical."

Fun? Magical?

Pickle took a few minutes to think it over. "Okay, Santa, I'm willing to try," he said.

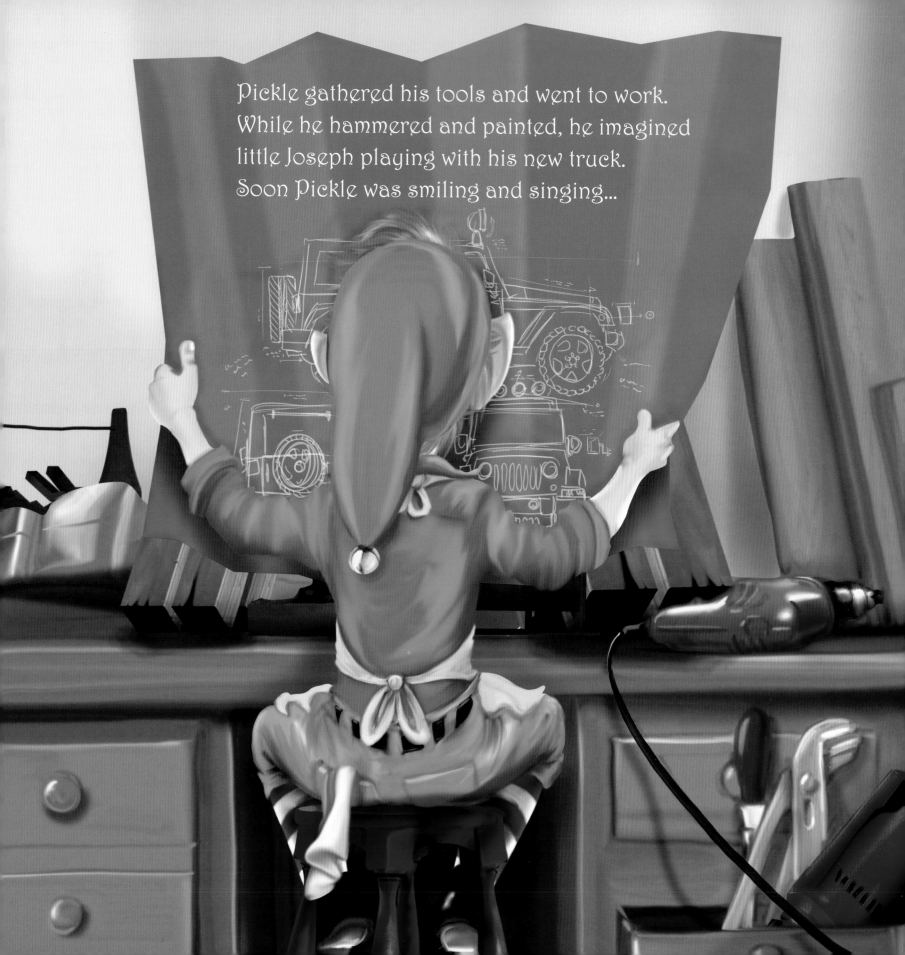

Pickle gathered his tools and went to work.
While he hammered and painted, he imagined
little Joseph playing with his new truck.
Soon Pickle was smiling and singing...

When Pickle was finished, he showed Santa.
"The other elves said it couldn't be done, but I
made the doors open and the headlights work!"

"Sounds like you had fun," Santa said, smiling.
"It's perfect."

Santa scooped Pickle into his lap.
"You see Pickle, this truck is perfect because you made it with your heart. That's what giving presents at Christmas time is all about."

Pickle jumped down.
"I'm ready to pick another wish!" Pickle declared.
"I have a really big heart."
Santa laughed loudly. "Next year, I promise."

On Christmas Eve, the elves gathered to see Santa off.
"Tonight," Santa said, "I have something very
important to give you."
Santa slowly opened his hand.
"A pickle?" the elves called out in surprise.

"A new Christmas tradition," Santa explained.

"In honor of Pickle Elf, our new holiday tradition will be a Christmas morning game for all to share; a way to remember that giving is fun and magical."

Pickle took a bow.

Tonight, leave the pickle by the milk and cookies so I can hide it on the North Pole Christmas tree," Santa explained. "Once everyone gathers on Christmas morning, the search for the pickle will begin. The lucky elf who finds it will open the first present—an extra gift just from me."

The elves cheered!

The elves followed Mrs. Claus outside.
"No peeking or sneaking tonight!"
she warned.
"I'm going find it!" Pickle declared.

Mrs. Claus smiled. "You might.
But if you don't, there's always next
year—and every Christmas to come."

"Remember, my elves, the true magic of Christmas can't be found under the tree. It's in your heart."

"I wish I could go with him," Pickle said.
The head elf agreed. "It must be magical to fly
around the world."
"Of course," Pickle said, smiling. "But watching
Joseph open my truck on Christmas morning...
now that would be truly magical."

In loving memory of Lucile Fitzpatrick

To my husband, Joe.
Thank you for letting me dream. I love you.

Special thanks to...
Jane Simons—Executive Director, Melinda Engel—CooperHudson PR,
Stephanie Bart-Horvath—Art Director, Liz Choi—GiveMeFive.com,
Simone Kaplan—Editor, Scott Conover—Graphic Artist and Box Designer,
Catie Wilson—Story Developer, Juliana Weiss-Roessler—Writing, Copy Editor,
Andrea H. Curley—Copy Editor

© 2014 The Christmas Pickle Tradition, LLC
First edition, first printing
ISBN: 978-0-615-92623-0
Printed and bound in China. This book is printed with vegetable inks.
http://ps.ppa.org/PickleBook14   Five Thousand Forms

For information regarding ordering or bulk discounts, please visit
www.ChristmasPickleTradition.com or contact Sales@PickleElf.com.